# Time to Read

## Nonfiction Stories for Grade 2

# Time to Read: Grade 2 Nonfiction Stories

**Reading Consultant**
Dr. Timothy Rasinski,
  Kent State University

**Photo Research**
TIME For Kids

**Managing Editor**
Dona Herweck Rice

**Editor-in-Chief**
Sharon Coan, M.S. Ed.

**Creative Director**
Lee Aucoin

**Publisher**
Rachelle Cracchiolo, M.S. Ed.

**_Teacher Created Materials, Inc._**
5301 Oceanus Drive
Huntington Beach, CA 92649

**ISBN 978-1-4333-0378-4**
*©2008 Teacher Created Materials, Inc.*

Printed at R.R.Donnelley & Sons
Crawfordsville, Indiana
April 2010

# Table of Contents

# A Visit to
# a Farm

## D. M. Rice

# Table of Contents

# Going to the Farm

Last summer, my brother and I visited my grandparents' farm. Our dad drove us there. He gave me a camera so I could make a book about our visit.

# Grandma and Grandpa

Grandma and Grandpa were there to meet us, along with their dog, Buddy.

They were all happy to see us.

← Buddy

Me →

Things I found

After our dad left, Grandma asked us, "What would you like to see?" We said, "Everything!"

So Grandma, Grandpa, and Buddy showed us the farm.

# The Barn and Silos

The barn.

First, we saw the big, red barn. The barn is big so that the animals and farm machines can fit inside.

Grandpa said that he milks the cows in the barn and keeps his tractor there, too.

The Silos

Next to the barn are tall silos.

The silos store the grain from the farm. The grain feeds the animals in the winter.

Grandpa's

## The Animals

Next, we saw the horse corral. Horses and ponies were there. They were standing nose to nose. They looked like they were talking to each other.

orses

One horse was near the fence.

Grandpa gave my brother a carrot to feed the horse. He ate that carrot right out of my brother's hand!

Kenny fee

a horse

The cows

Beyond the corral, we
saw the cows in the pasture.
Some were eating and some
were just standing.

A calf drinks milk.

One small calf was getting milk from its mother.

# The Fields

Harvesting the grain

When we left the pasture, I heard a low roar. I asked Grandpa, "What is that noise?" He said, "It is one of the farm machines. Come and see."

Grandpa and Grandma took us to the wheat fields.

wheat

19

A man was driving a large machine.

The combine

Grandpa said that it was a combine used to harvest the grain.

We waved to the man.
He waved back. Then
Buddy barked and wagged
his tail. He was waving, too!

| | |
|---|---|
| | Barn |
| | Farmhouse |
| | Silo |
| | Wheat |
| | Pasture |
| | Trees |

Farm Map

Our grandparents' farm is big. Here is a map of the farm. Maybe one day you can visit, too.

# Glossary

barn

combine

corral

pasture

silo

tractor

# A Visit to an
# Automobile Factory

## D. M. Rice

# Table of Contents

# Going to the Factory

One morning my dad woke me up early.

"Surprise!" he said. "You are coming to work with me."

My friend
Angie →

My dad has
the best job
ever. He works
in an automobile
factory. They
make cars there.

**Did you know?**
Automobile is another word for car.

# Engineers

My dad is an engineer. That means he helps to plan how a car will look and work.

Dad works with other engineers. They work together so the car will be safe and run great.

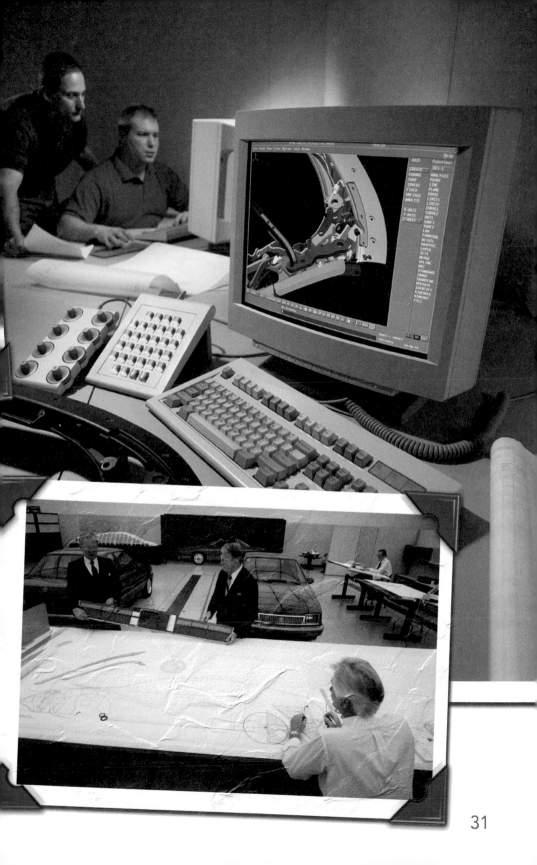

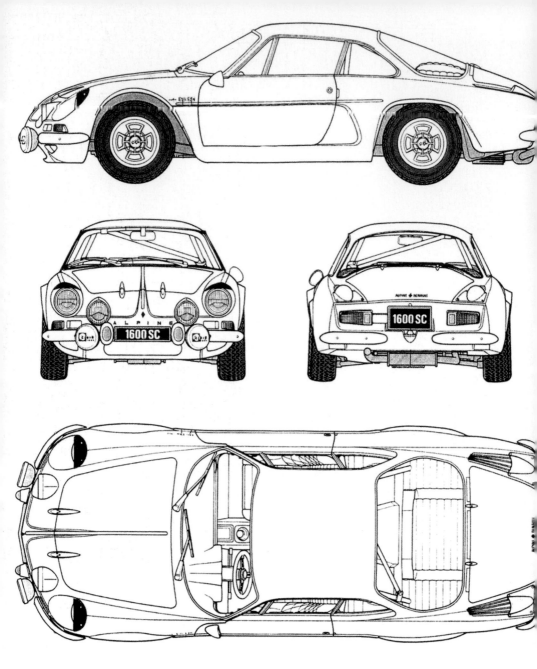

Dad and his team draw
their plans. They look like
this.

I want to be an engineer,
too. So, I draw my own plans.

# Getting the Parts

When the plans are ready, the car can be built. But first, factory workers must make or buy all the parts for the car. There are hundreds of parts!

A car needs springs, brakes, and a steering wheel. It needs pistons, valves, and more.

It is not easy to build a car!

# Assembly

Once they have the parts, workers can put the car together. This is called assembly.

They work in teams. Each team builds a different part of

the car. One team builds the
engine. Another builds the
body. Another is in charge of
the wheels and tires.

There are many teams
with many different jobs.
All of them are important.

Each team checks its work
carefully. They want the

people who drive the car to be safe.

Engineers check the work, too.

# Ready for Sale

When the cars are ready, they go to a shipping yard. The shipping yard sends them to dealers. Sometimes the cars go by boat. Sometimes they go by truck. Then people buy the cars from the dealers.

When I see cars on the road, I feel proud of my dad. He makes good cars for people to enjoy.

When I grow up, I'm going to work at the automobile factory, too!

# How a Car Is Made

How is a car made?
This chart will show you.

Plans are drawn for a new car.

Parts are made for the car.

The car is put together by teams.

The car is checked and tested.

The finished car is sent to the shipping yard.

The shipping yard sends the car to a dealer.

People buy the car from the dealer.

# Glossary

assembly

automobile

dealer

engineer

shipping yard

# MEXICO

## Ginger McDonnell

# Table of Contents

# Welcome to Mexico!

*Hola!* Welcome to Mexico!

Mexico is a big country. Everywhere you go there is something new to see.

Here is a wide, blue sky
over a warm, brown desert.
A rattlesnake lies in the sun.

U.S.A.

Rio Bravo del Norte

Mexico

Here a rancher drives his cattle across the plains. They are going to the *Rio Bravo del Norte*. It is a long and winding river.

Along the coast, the mighty
ocean roars.

In the mountain forests, a bear family searches for food.

Yes, there is something different wherever you go in Mexico.

# Animals

Many animals call Mexico home. Have you ever seen a puma? You might see one in Mexico.

Coyotes also live there. You might hear a coyote howling at the Mexican moon.

Lizards, snakes, turtles, and seals are some other animals you can find there. These are just a few of Mexico's animals.

# Plants

Many different plants live in Mexico, too. Cactuses grow in the deserts. Some look like people reaching to the sky.

Jungle vines and plants grow thickly in parts of Mexico. In other parts, deep forests of oak and pine trees are found.

# The Land

Mexico is known for its sunny coasts. People go there to enjoy the sand and ocean waves.

Fishermen work along the coasts. They catch some of the world's best fish. Have you tried a fish taco? Tasty!

In from the coasts,
mountains surround most of
Mexico. Wild animals roam the
forests there.

Much of Mexico is covered
in desert plains. The land is dry,
but many plants and animals
find a way to live.

# More About Mexico

Some old, old buildings can be found in Mexico. There are even pyramids there! People come from around the world to see them.

Mexico's true name is the United Mexican States. In Mexico, the people say *Estados Unidos Mexicanos*.

Mexico City is the capital of Mexico. You can find museums, universities, and tall office buildings in the city.

What else would you like to know about Mexico? This chart will tell you more important facts.

# MEXICAN FACTS

| | |
|---|---|
| Official Language: | Spanish |
| Leader: | president |
| Number of States: | 31 |
| Flag:  | 3 stripes (green, white, red); eagle, snake, and a cactus symbol in the middle |
| Independence Day: | September 16 |
| Major Religion: | Roman Catholic |
| Major crops: | corn, sugar, wheat, oranges, coffee |
| Money: | nuevo peso |

# Glossary

cactus

cattle

coast

desert

jungle

ocean

plain

pyramid

# THE CARIBBEAN

## Ginger McDonnell

# Table of Contents

# Welcome to the Caribbean!

Welcome to the Caribbean! Many people call this place paradise.

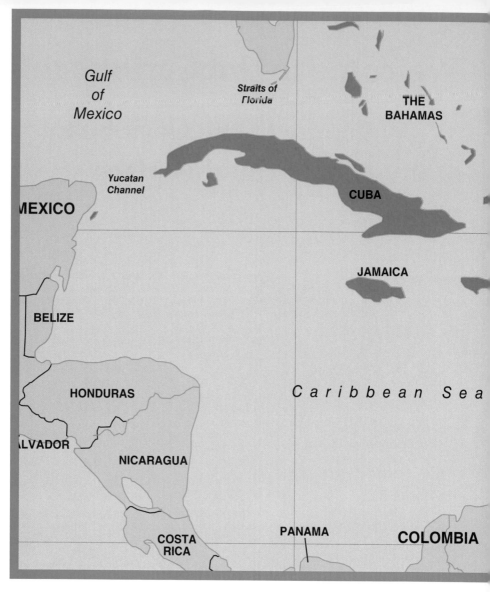

The Caribbean Sea is a big, beautiful sea filled with hundreds of tropical islands. The water is warm and colorful. The islands are alive with beauty.

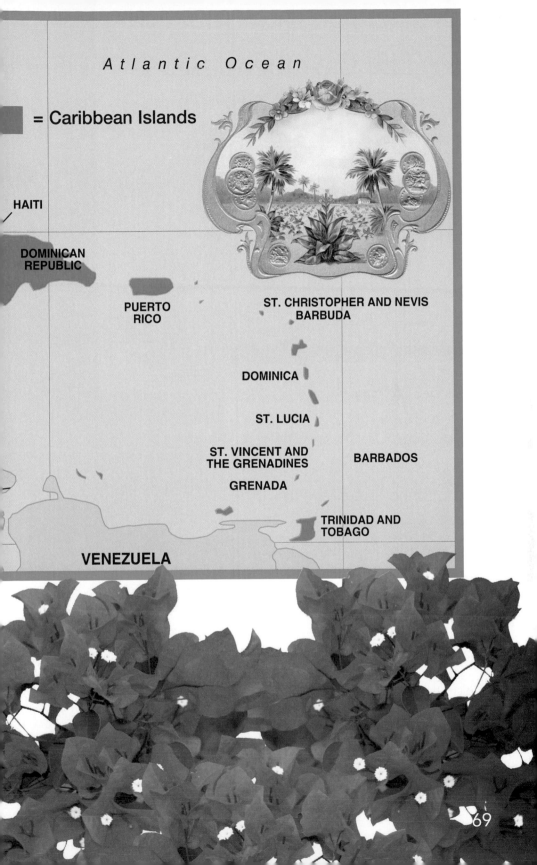

Atlantic Ocean

█ = Caribbean Islands

HAITI

DOMINICAN
REPUBLIC

PUERTO
RICO

ST. CHRISTOPHER AND NEVIS
BARBUDA

DOMINICA

ST. LUCIA

ST. VINCENT AND
THE GRENADINES

BARBADOS

GRENADA

TRINIDAD AND
TOBAGO

VENEZUELA

69

The Caribbean Sea is part of the Atlantic Ocean. It is about 1,500 miles across and 900 miles wide. That's a big sea!

## Pirates?

Does the Caribbean make you think of pirates? Pirate ships like this one really did sail the seas long ago.

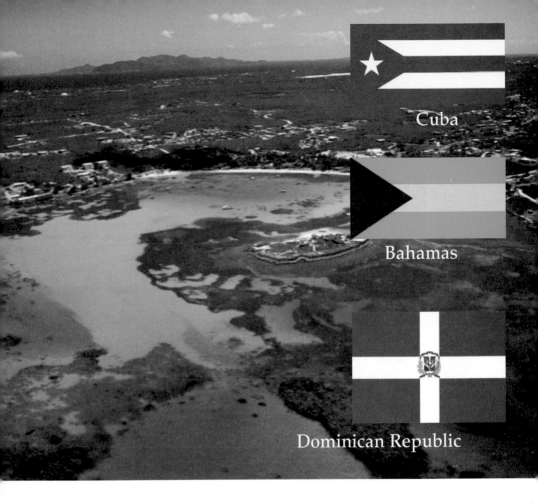

Cuba

Bahamas

Dominican Republic

For many years, countries around the world wanted to control the Caribbean. They fought over the islands. Now some islands belong to other countries, but some islands are their own countries.

# Animals

Many birds live in the Caribbean area. There are hundreds of kinds there! Birds such as gulls, macaws, and flamingoes like Caribbean weather.

Tortoises, snakes, and caymans are three of the reptiles living in the Caribbean area. Caymans are like crocodiles, but they are shorter with smaller snouts.

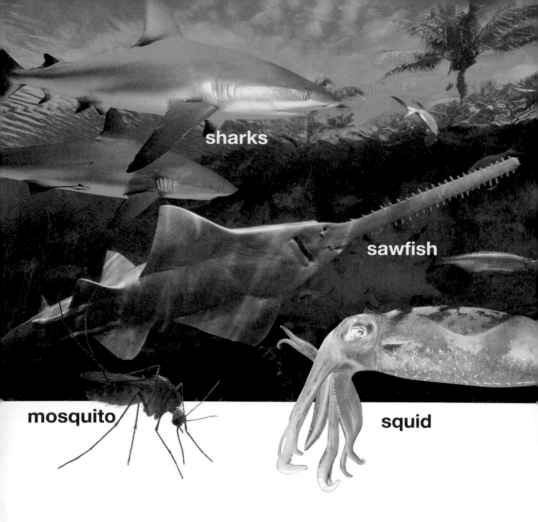

sharks

sawfish

mosquito

squid

Not many land mammals are native to the Caribbean, but many sea animals are. Sharks, tuna, crabs, and eels are just a few.

There are many insects, too. Watch out for pesky mosquitoes!

# Plants

The islands of the Caribbean are green with plant life. They are colorful, too. Big and bright fruits and flowers grow everywhere.

Palm trees grow all over the Caribbean islands. People can sit on sandy beaches watching the tall palms swaying in the winds.

There are other trees, too, but the Caribbean is known mainly for its palms.

# More About the Caribbean

fairy basslet

butterfly fish

The Caribbean is a great place for vacations. People can sail and swim in the beautiful water. With a snorkel, they can watch fish and coral gardens up close.

squirrel fish

angelfish

butterfly fish

blowfish or porcupine fish

## Steel Drums

While on vacation, people can enjoy Caribbean music, too. The special sound of Caribbean music is made with a steel drum. Steel drums were first made from big oil drums that were thrown away.

People like the Caribbean
sunsets.  Sunsets there are worth
the trip!

Many of the cities in the
Caribbean islands were built
before cars were invented. So,
roads can be narrow. They are
just right for walking.

The Caribbean is one of the most popular tourist spots in the world. On many of the islands, more people visit each year than live there.

What else would you like to know about the Caribbean Sea? This chart will tell you more important facts.

# Caribbean Sea Facts

**Depth:** between about 6,000 and 12,000 feet

**Borders:** West Indies (north and east), Central America (west), South America and Panama (south)

**Name:** came from the Carib people in the 15$^{th}$ century

**Number of Islands:** hundreds

**Major Islands:** Anguilla, Antigua, Aruba, Bahamas, Barbados, Bonaire, British Virgin Islands, Cayman Islands, Cuba, Curaçao, Dominica, Dominican Republic, Grenada, Guadeloupe, Guyana, Haiti, Jamaica, Martinique, Puerto Rico, Saba, St. Barthelemy, St. Eustatius, St. Kitts, St. Lucia, St. Martin, St. Vincent and The Grenadines, Trinidad and Tobago, Turks and Caicos, U. S. Virgin Islands.

# Glossary

**paradise**  a beautiful and perfect place

**pesky**  bothersome and annoying

**snouts**  long animal noses that stick out

**snorkel**  a hose used for breathing when a person is underwater

**tropical**  from areas of land near Earth's equator where the weather is warm and wet

**tourist**  a person who is on vacation and visiting a place away from home to see the sights

# VOLCANOES

## Cy Armour

# Table of Contents

# Volcano!

Long ago, people thought that powerful gods lived inside volcanoes. When the gods were angry, they would spit fire, ash, and lava onto the land.

Today, we know that
volcanoes are a part of nature.

The word **volcano** comes from *Vulcan*, the Roman god of fire.

But why do volcanoes happen?

# Why Volcanoes Happen

A volcano starts as a big, deep hole or crack in the earth. When pressure builds, ash, rock, gas, and **magma** escape through the hole. In time, the escaped material can form a mountain.

**What Is It?**
**Magma** (MAG-mə) is hot melted rock.

Why does this happen?

The earth is made of layers. The outside layer is the **crust**. The crust is made of big pieces of land called **plates**. The plates move slowly against one another.

Under the crust is the **mantle**. It is a thick, hot layer of rock. Deep inside the earth, it is so hot the rock melts into magma.

Pressure and heat in the mantle push the magma into a **magma chamber**. Magma is lighter than the crust, so it tries to push above it.

Crust

Magma
Chamber

Mantle

Finally, pressure from gases pushes the magma through the crust. This is called an **eruption**.

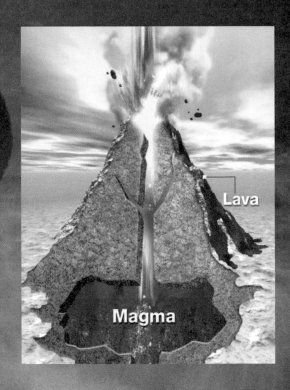

Magma

Lava

Plate edges are the best places for magma to escape. But if plates are thin enough, magma can push through other holes and cracks in the earth's crust.

# Eruption!

An eruption happens when magma, ash, rock, and gases are released from a volcano. Sometimes an eruption comes in a blast. Sometimes it comes in a slow ooze.

If a volcano might erupt, it is called **active**. If we think it will not erupt now or in the future, it is called **dormant** (DOR-mənt). Dormant is another word for asleep.

Think what happens when you shake a can of soda. When you open it, the soda might blast out or just overflow down the sides. It depends on how much pressure has built up.

The more pressure, the
bigger the blast!

Once outside the volcano, magma is called **lava**. Lava can be fast and runny or slow and thick. Either way, the lava is hot, hot, hot! It can be as hot as 2012°F.

# Where Are Volcanoes?

Pinatubo, Philippines

Mt. Fugi, Japan

Mt. Merapi, Java

Mauna Loa, Hawai

NORTH AMERICA

AUSTRALIA

*Pacific Ocean*

There are hundreds of volcanoes all over the world. More than half of them are along the shores of the Pacific Ocean. They are called the Ring of Fire.

Mt. St. Helens, Washington

EUROPE

Mt. Etna, Italy

Atlantic Ocean

AFRICA

Indian Ocean

SOUTH AMERICA

**KEY**

▲ Active Volcano

Ring of Fire

Mid-Atlantic Ridge

Another large group of volcanoes is found under the Atlantic Ocean. It is called the Mid-Atlantic Ridge. It is the largest mountain range in the world!

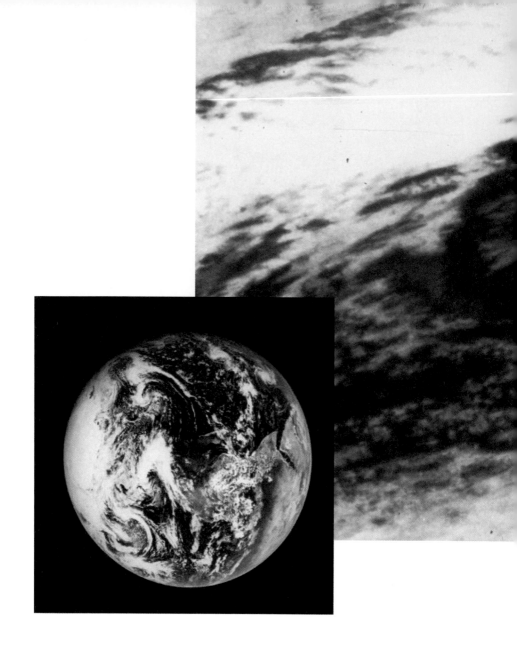

Earth is not the only place
where volcanoes are found.
They are on other planets, too.

In fact, the largest volcano
we know is Olympus Mons on
Mars. It is 16 miles tall and as
wide as all of Arizona.

Now that's a big volcano!

# Glossary

**crust**   the top layer of Earth

**eruption**   the release of magma, ash, rock, and gases from a volcano

**lava**   magma that is outside a volcano

**magma**   hot, liquid rock

**magma chamber**   a pocket within a volcano where magma collects before erupting

**mantle**   a thick layer of Earth below the crust that is made of gas and magma

**plates**   large sections of Earth's crust that move, sliding together and apart

**pressure**   force that builds and pushes against something

**volcano**   areas of land where magma from inside Earth is pushed to the surface and out in an eruption

# Snakes

## Christopher Blazeman

# Table of Contents

# Sammy

"Mom, can I keep him?" you ask.

"Keep who?" she says.

"Sammy," you answer.

"Who is Sammy?" she asks.

"Sssssss," Sammy hisses.

"Ahhhh!" she screams.

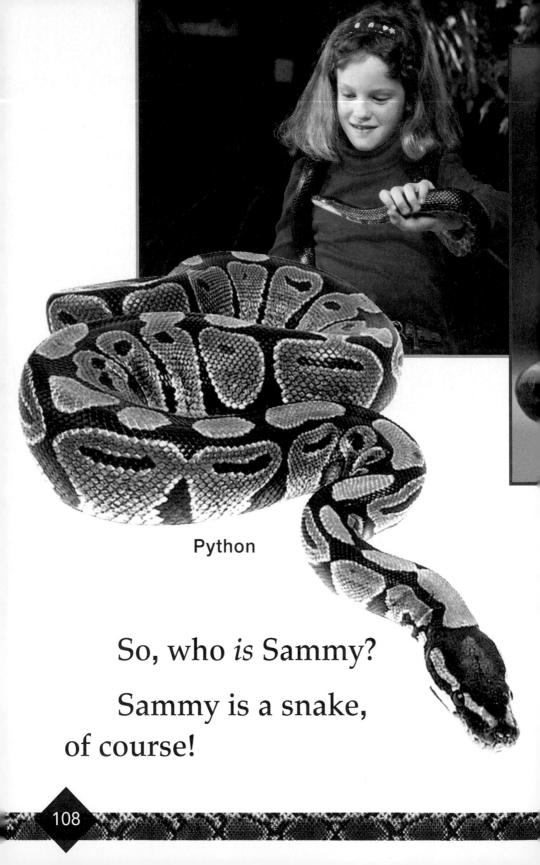

Python

So, who *is* Sammy?

Sammy is a snake,
of course!

Would a snake make a good pet? This book will tell you about snakes. When you have finished, you can decide for yourself. But be sure you ask before you bring one home!

# All About Snakes

Albin-
Pytho

Some snakes are as long as
a tree. Some are as short as a
finger. Some are thick, and some
are thin. Some are dangerous,
but most are harmless.

Grass Snake

Boa Constrictor

Snakes can be different. But they are the same in many ways, too.

Snakes are reptiles. Most snakes lay tough, leathery eggs. When a baby snake is born, it does not need its mother's care. It can take care of itself.

King Snake

Scales cover the bodies of snakes. They look wet and slimy, but they are really dry and hard.

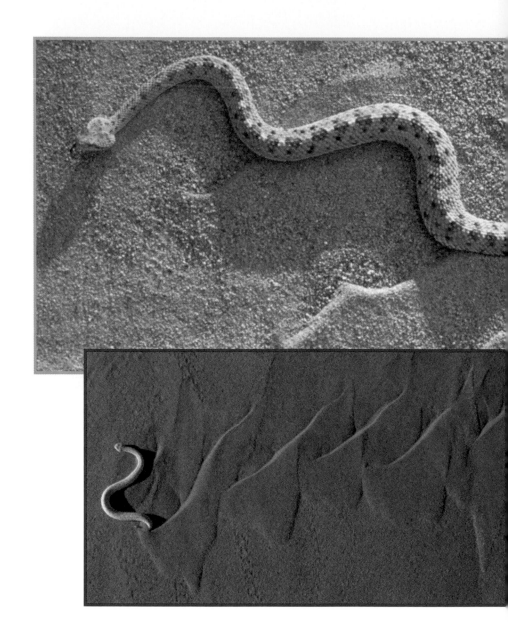

Snakes have no legs. They must glide on their bellies or wiggle from side to side.

Snakes have no eyelids. No problem! Most snakes see well anyway.

forked tongue

Snakes do not have ears. They feel movement on the ground. That is their way of hearing.

Can snakes smell? Yes, with the help of their forked tongues!

Coral Snake

Boa Constrictor

Snakes are cold-blooded. Their body heat depends on the heat around them. That is why most snakes live in warm places.

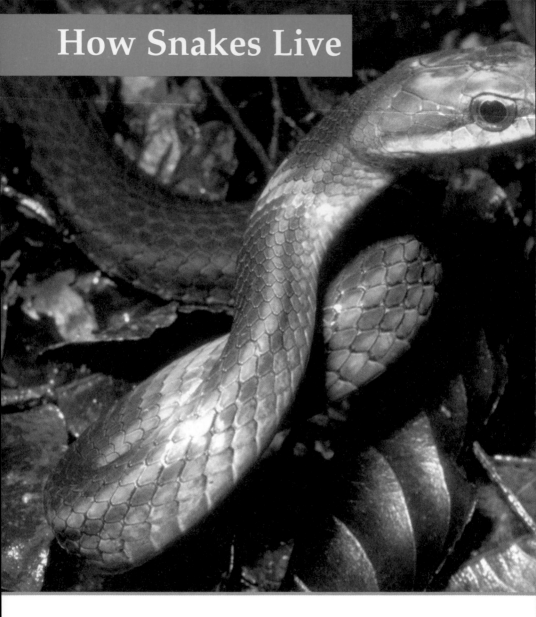

Even so, you can find snakes everywhere. Snakes may live in jungles, swamps, forests, and deserts.

Banana
Viper

Water Moccasin

They may live in trees, lakes, or holes in the ground.

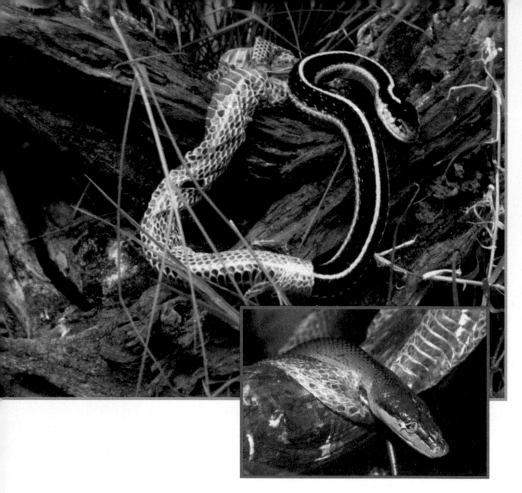

Even if you do not know where a snake lives, you can tell where one has been. Snakes shed their skin as they grow. The skin peels off like a sock. Then the snake crawls away, leaving its skin behind.

Rattlesnake

rattle

Sometimes snakes let you know where they are. They may rattle their tails or make noises to frighten you away.

Albino Cobra

Some snakes play dead to protect themselves. Others have bright colors to show that they are poisonous.

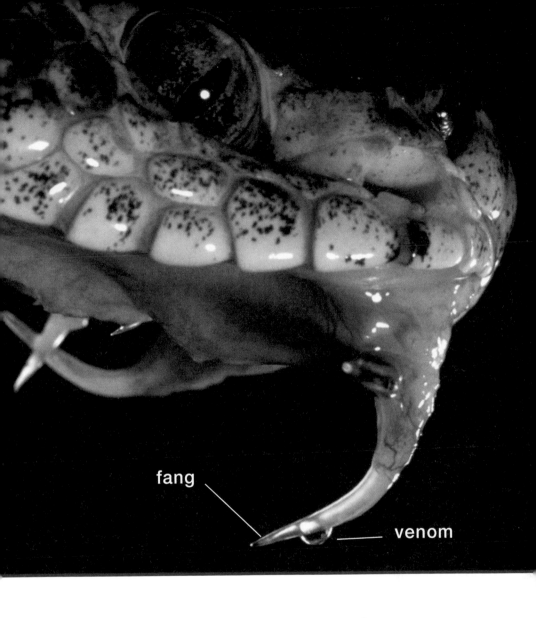

fang

venom

Snake poison is called **venom**. Venom flows through the hollow, sharp **fangs** of some snakes. They use venom to stop other animals.

Anaconda

Since all snakes eat meat, venom helps some of them get their food. Others squeeze their food until it dies.

Snakes swallow their food whole. Sometimes it is still alive!

Usually snakes eat small animals. Some snakes have hinges on their jaws to open wide and eat large animals, too.

So, will a snake make a good pet? There is no right answer. You must decide for yourself.

To help you decide, here is a chart to remind you all about snakes.

# SNAKE CHART

| | |
|---|---|
| eyes | two eyes, but no eyelids |
| ears | no ears, so feel movement instead |
| bodies | covered with scales, have no legs, are cold-blooded, and shed skin |
| movement | glide or wiggle |
| babies | hatch from eggs or born live, and can take care of themselves |
| protection | rattle, make noises, play dead, have bright colors, or shoot venom |
| eating | bite or squeeze and swallow whole |
| living place | jungles, swamps, forests, deserts, trees, lakes, or holes in the ground |

# Glossary

**cold-blooded**  having body heat that depends on the heat around you

**fangs**  long, pointed teeth

**hinges**  joints that allow snakes to open their jaws very wide

**scales**  hard, dry plates that cover the bodies of snakes

**squeeze**  to crush tightly; for snakes, this is also called *constriction*

**venom**  poison that flows through the hollow fangs of some snakes

# All About
# Chocolate

## Madison Spielman

# Table of Contents

# Chocolate Dreams

Close your eyes and imagine your favorite chocolate candy. Think about how it smells. Think about the taste. Think how it melts in your mouth.

Mmmmm! Are you ready for some chocolate now?

If you are like most people in the United States, you love chocolate, and you eat about twelve pounds of it each year!

# The First Chocolate

Chocolate started out a very long time ago as a type of drink made in South America. But hard chocolate that people can eat was not made until much later.

cacao beans

cacao pod

People long ago did not have chocolate. Chocolate like we have today was not made until 1828.

In that year, a Dutch chemist removed the cocoa butter from cocoa beans. Cocoa butter tastes bitter.

Without the cocoa butter, cocoa powder was left. Cocoa powder is the delicious beginning of chocolate.

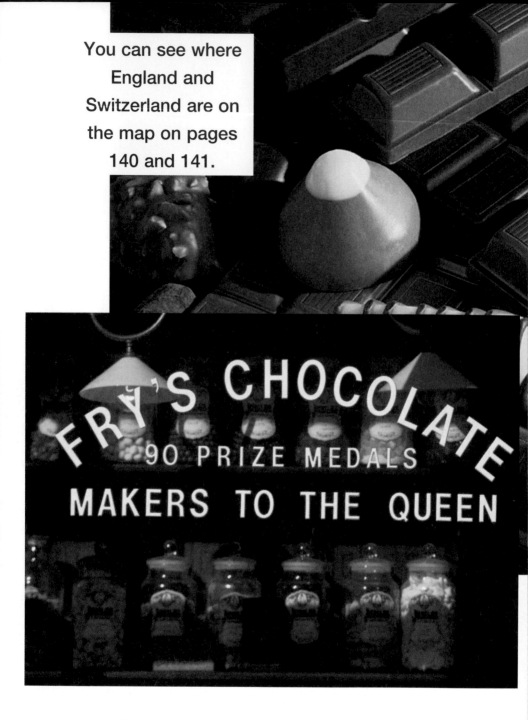

You can see where England and Switzerland are on the map on pages 140 and 141.

The first solid chocolate was sold in England in 1847.

In 1875, a Swiss man added milk to chocolate and made the first milk chocolate. That is the kind of chocolate in most candy today.

# Where Does Chocolate Come From?

Chocolate is made from the seeds of the **cacao** tree. The seeds grow inside pods. They are called cocoa beans.

Cacao (kuh-KAY-oh) comes from the Latin word that means "food of the gods."

They should really be called cacao beans. But long ago, English speaking people spelled cacao wrong by mistake. People have just kept it that way.

England

Arctic Ocean

Beaufort Sea

Greenland Sea

Baffin Bay

Norwegian Sea

Hudson Bay

Labrador Sea

North Sea

North Atlantic Ocean

English Channel

Bay of Biscay

Black

North Atlantic Ocean

Mediterranean Sea

Gulf of Mexico

Caribbean Sea

GHANA

NIGERIA

IVORY COAST

The Equator

BRAZIL

South Atlantic Ocean

## Key

where cocoa come from

where hard chocolate was first made

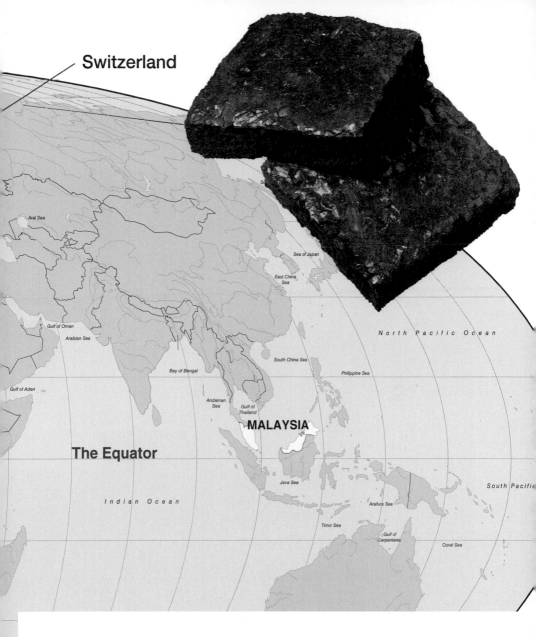

Switzerland

Aral Sea

Sea of Japan

East China Sea

Gulf of Oman

Arabian Sea

North Pacific Ocean

South China Sea

Bay of Bengal

Philippine Sea

Gulf of Aden

Andaman Sea

Gulf of Thailand

**MALAYSIA**

**The Equator**

Java Sea

South Pacific

Indian Ocean

Arafura Sea

Timor Sea

Gulf of Carpentaria

Coral Sea

Most of the world's cocoa beans come from countries in South America, Africa, and Asia. Look at the map to find them.

# How Is Chocolate Made?

It takes time and work to make good chocolate.

Ferment means
to change slowly.
Yeast and bacteria
can cause this
chemical change.

First, the cacao pods must
be picked. Then they are
**fermented** for six days.

When they are ready, the pods are split open. The seeds are removed and dried.

They are dried in the sun for about seven days. Sometimes they are dried in special machines instead.

Next, the dried beans are
sent to chocolate factories.

There the cocoa butter is removed, and the seeds are roasted and ground into powder.

The powder is mixed with sugar, milk, or other ingredients to make different kinds of chocolate.

Next, the chocolate is heated in a special machine called a **conche**. The best chocolate is heated there for at least one week.

A **conche** (conch) keeps the chocolate liquid and smooth.

Finally, the chocolate is cooled slowly, warmed again, and cooled to its final hardness. Now, it is ready to be packaged and sent to stores where you can buy and eat it!

# Who Loves Chocolate?

People in the United States eat almost half of all the chocolate eaten in the world.

But it is the Swiss people who love it best. The average person there eats twenty-two pounds of chocolate each year!

In fact, many people think that Swiss chocolate is the best chocolate in the world.

# Chocolate, Chocolate Everywhere!

Is chocolate only in candies? No! You can find chocolate in many different foods. Chocolate cake, pudding, cookies, ice cream, and hot cocoa are just a few of them. Wherever you find food, you can probably find some kind of chocolate, too.

What is your favorite chocolate food?

# Glossary

cacao beans

cacao pod

cacao tree

candies

cocoa powder

conche

# In the Forest

## Howard Rice

# Table of Contents

Cardinal

# A Magical Place

Leaves of all colors and shapes crackle under your feet as you walk. The crisp, blue sky peeks through a blanket of branches above you. Woodland animals scurry to their nests and dens.

No wonder so many fairy tale characters live in the forest! The forest is a magical place.

A woods is a small forest.

# What Are Forests?

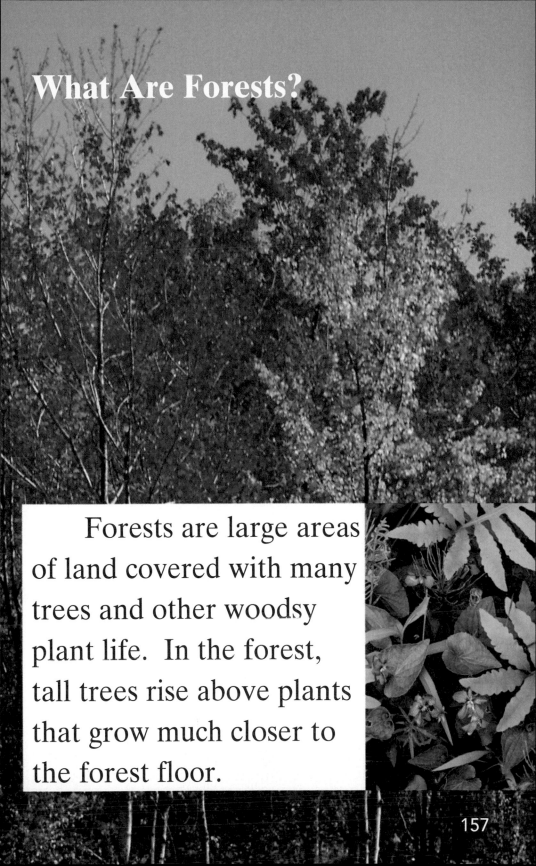

Forests are large areas of land covered with many trees and other woodsy plant life. In the forest, tall trees rise above plants that grow much closer to the forest floor.

Did you know that there is more than one kind of forest?

Some forests grow trees whose leaves change color in the autumn. The leaves fall to the ground in the winter. Then the trees rest until new leaves grow in the spring.

In other forests, evergreen trees grow. The leaves of most evergreen trees do not change color and fall away. These trees stay green all year long.

Trees that grow needles need less water than trees that grow other kinds of leaves.

Some evergreen trees grow needles for leaves. They also grow cones.

One pine tree in Nevada is the oldest living thing on Earth. It is 4,700 years old!

Squirrel

The cones have seeds inside them to grow new trees. But watch out! Squirrels like to eat the seeds before they have a chance to grow.

Another kind of forest is called a rainforest. As you can guess, a rainforest gets a lot of water. Trees and plants there are very green and moist.

But not all rainforests get a lot of rain. Sometimes they get a lot of fog and moist air instead. The fog brings the water they need to help the trees grow.

# Where Are They?

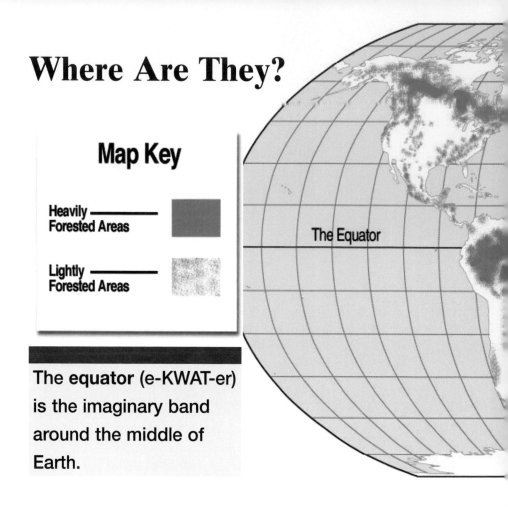

**Map Key**

Heavily ———— Forested Areas

Lightly ———— Forested Areas

The Equator

The **equator** (e-KWAT-er) is the imaginary band around the middle of Earth.

Forests can be found all over the world, but the kind of forest depends on where it is.

Forests that change color are found in many places, but mainly in the eastern United States, Canada, Europe, Russia, China, and Japan.

166

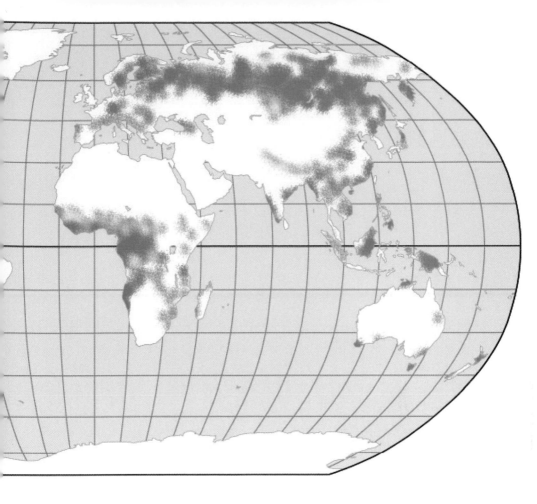

Forests filled with cone and needle trees are only in the north.

Many rainforests are near Earth's **equator**. Other rainforests are near coasts, mainly in the northwest United States.

# Animals in the Forest

Raccoon

Red Fox

Different kinds of forests have different kinds of animals, too.

In the forests where leaves change color and fall, you might see raccoons and squirrels hunting for nuts. You might see deer in a clearing or black bears peeking

Turkey

Black Bear

around trees. Foxes, turkeys, skunks, and rabbits may be nearby.

During the winter, these forests are much quieter. Many animals hibernate or go to warmer places when it gets cold.

Wolf

Bobcat

In the evergreen forests where needles and cones grow on trees, moose and wolves roam the land. Beavers build their dams, and great

Gray Owl

Moose

Beaver

gray owls hoot from the trees. If
you look quickly, you might see a
lynx running beneath the branches.

Rainbow Lorikeet

Poison Dart Frogs

Tree Frog

Rainforests have animals, too. In fact, there are so many animals that the rainforest can be a very noisy place! Monkeys chatter as they swing from vines. Colorful

Humboldts Night Monkey

Spider Monkey

How many plants and animals are in the woods? There are millions of species!

birds call to each other from the trees and sky. Bright green, red, and orange frogs ribbit as they hop along the ground.

# Dangers to the Forest

Forests are an important part of our world, but many things are a danger to them. Fires sometimes burn down forests as far as you can see. Insects and sickness can spread

Forests are important! We get the oxygen we need from trees and plants. They give us lumber, food, and medicines, too.

Tar Spots

Bark Beetle

through trees and kill them. Then animals die, too, because they need the trees and plants to live.

We need our forests, so we must take care of them.

# Glossary

autumn

cones

evergreen

needles

rainforest

# OUR EARTH

## Kenneth Walsh

# Table of Contents

# A Big and Mighty Planet

Have you ever played in the dirt? Maybe it was warm and sandy and you let it sift through your fingers. Maybe it was cool and muddy and you shaped it like clay.

Either way, you did something pretty amazing.  You held one small part of a big and mighty planet in your hands. You held part of our planet, Earth.

# The Big, Blue Marble

Earth is part of our solar system. That means it is one of eight planets that **orbit** our sun. It is the third planet from the sun.

## From Sun to Earth

How far is Earth from the sun? 92,897,000 miles!

## In Orbit

To orbit means to move in the path of a circle or oval around an object. Earth moves about 45,000 miles per hour!

Something orbits Earth, too. It is our moon.

People say that from the moon, Earth looks like a big, blue marble.

# Water, Water Everywhere

Why does Earth seem blue from space? The reason is there is much more water than land on Earth's surface.

## Glaciers

A **glacier** (GLA-shər) is a large body of ice that spreads across an area of land or moves slowly down a hill or valley.

Water covers 70% of Earth's surface. Most of that water is in oceans. A small part is in lakes and rivers or frozen in **glaciers** and ice caps at Earth's north and south poles.

Water is important on Earth. It is the only planet in our solar system that holds living things, and every living thing needs water.

# Life on Other Planets?

Some other planets have water, but they do not have everything else that is needed for life, like comfortable temperatures and good air to breathe.

Water also changes Earth. Large amounts of water are very powerful. Rivers and glaciers cut into Earth's surface over time.

**Water Fact**

Earth's oceans are five times deeper than the average height of the land.

For example, the Colorado River slowly carved out the Grand Canyon over six million years!

# Earth's Atmosphere

There is something else just as important as water on Earth. It is air.

Air makes up Earth's **atmosphere**. The atmosphere is like a big, thick blanket wrapped around Earth. The air we breathe from the atmosphere is called **oxygen**.

## How Big?

Earth's **atmosphere** (AT-məs-fiər) reaches for hundreds of miles away from Earth's surface.

# Oxygen

**Oxygen** (AWK-si-jən) is an element in the air. We breathe it as a gas. It has no taste, color, or smell.  Oxygen is also part of water.

The atmosphere is also important because it protects life on Earth. It absorbs energy from the sun, and it blocks the sun's harmful rays.

Earth's atmosphere is made of several layers. Weather takes place in the layer nearest Earth, which is about 10 miles high.

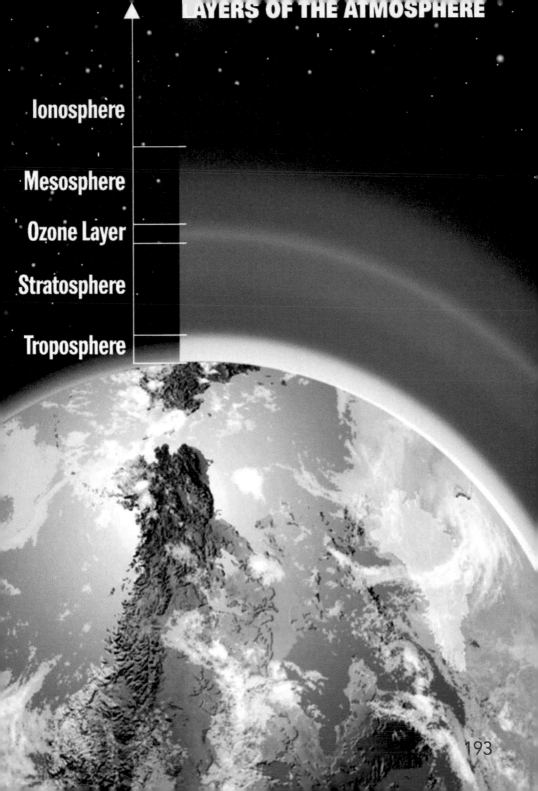

# LAYERS OF THE ATMOSPHERE

Ionosphere

Mesosphere

Ozone Layer

Stratosphere

Troposphere

# Inside the Earth

Earth is also made of several layers. The surface is called the crust. It is a cold, rocky layer about 60 miles deep. It is made of large pieces called plates that move and bump together, causing earthquakes, volcanoes, and other powerful activities.

Below the crust is the mantle. It is about 1,800 miles deep. It is made of hot, liquid rock and gas.

In Earth's center is the core. The core is more than 2,000 miles wide. The temperature there is so hot that it can reach as high as 12,000° F! How hot is that? The hottest day recorded on Earth's surface was just 136° F.

# Earth Layers

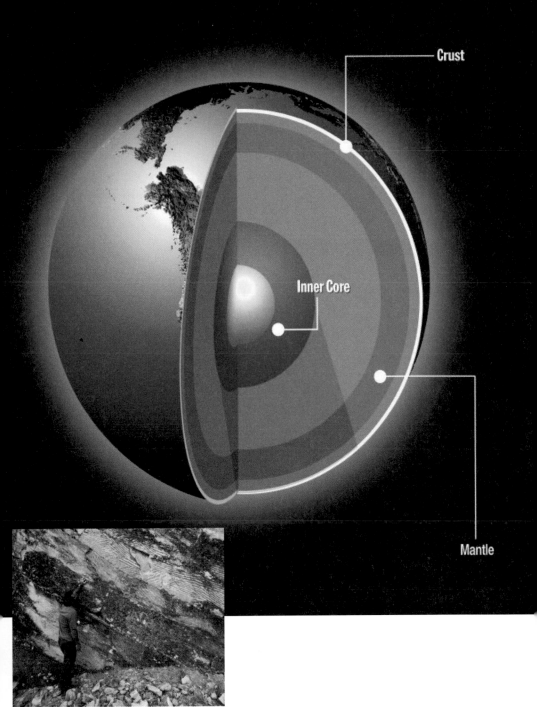

Crust

Inner Core

Mantle

Layers of rock in the crust

# Earth History

Scientists believe that Earth is about 4.65 billion years old.  At first, Earth was very hot and liquid.  There was no life.  That came much later.

The shape of Earth formed over time, too.  Slopes and valleys that exist today did not always exist.  Water and wind have shaped some.  Earth's movements have shaped others.

## Earth's Size

Compared to other things in space, how big is Earth?  Imagine this.  If the sun were the size of a soccer ball, Earth would be the size of a sunflower seed—without the shell!

People have changed Earth, too.
Roads, buildings, factories, and dams
change Earth. Pollution changes it, too,
but not for the better.

**Ball or Egg?**

Is Earth round like
a ball? No! It is
shaped slightly like
an egg.

Living things on Earth have also changed over time. Long ago, dinosaurs roamed. There are no dinosaurs now, but scientists think that some birds may be related to them.

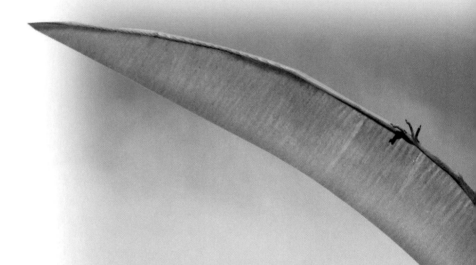

Plants and animals change over time. They change to become healthier and stronger.

Earth never stops changing. It is not the same today as it was when it began. Millions of years from now, it will not be the same as it is today.

California Gull
(modern bird)
Wingspan: 4 feet

Pteranodon
(flying dinosaur)
Wingspan: 25 feet

# Glossary

**atmosphere**  layers of air surrounding and protecting Earth

**core**  the hot center layer of Earth

**crust**  the cold, rocky surface layer of Earth

**mantle**  the hot, liquid, rock and gas, middle layer of Earth

**orbits**  moves in the path of a circle or oval around an object

**oxygen**  colorless, tasteless, and odorless gas in Earth's atmosphere that people breathe

**ozone layer**  layer of Earth's atmosphere that blocks out harmful rays

**plates**  sections of Earth's crust

**solar system**  a group of planets and other heavenly bodies that move around a central sun

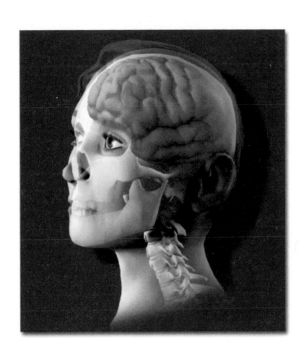

# The Brain

## Ben Williams

# Table of Contents

# The World's Fastest Computer

There is an amazing computer. It is faster than any other computer in the world. It can understand speech and writing. It can come up with new ideas. It can make plans. It can control a whole, complicated system and do many things at once without shutting down.

In fact, the more it is used, the better it seems to get.

What is this
amazing computer?  It
is your brain, of course!

## Superbrain!

How fast is your brain? Some people say that it can handle 10 quadrillion instructions each second. That's 10,000,000,000,000,000!

# What Is a Brain?

Most animals have a brain. But your brain—the human brain—is the most amazing brain of all. It is larger and more complicated than other brains.

The human brain sits inside the skull at the top and back of the head. It is about the size of a small cauliflower, and it is shaped a little like one, too.

The brain is very important. That is why it is protected inside the hard skull bones.

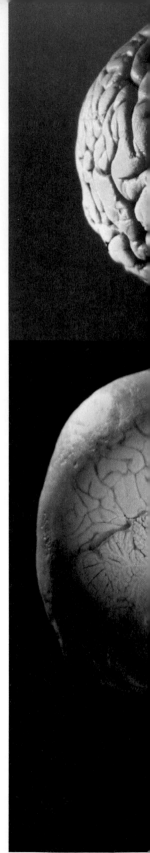

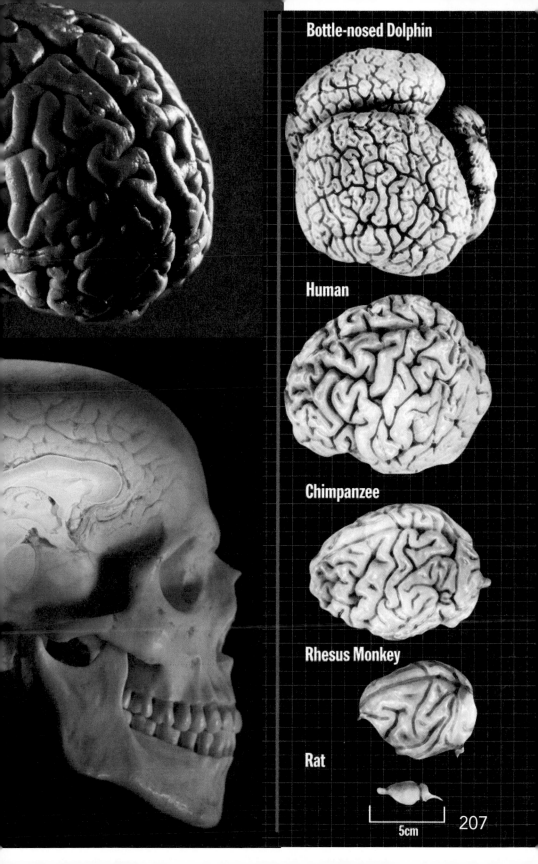

Bottle-nosed Dolphin

Human

Chimpanzee

Rhesus Monkey

Rat

5cm

207

Touch your finger to your nose. Clap your hands. Sing a song. You can do all of these things because your brain tells your body what to do.

Your brain is always on the job. It is like a boss and all the parts of your body are the workers. All you have to do is

think a thought, and your brain makes the workers get right to work.

For example, if you want to run, your brain thinks, "Run," and your legs and feet do their jobs. If you want to eat, your brain sends a message to all the right parts. Just like that, you are eating.

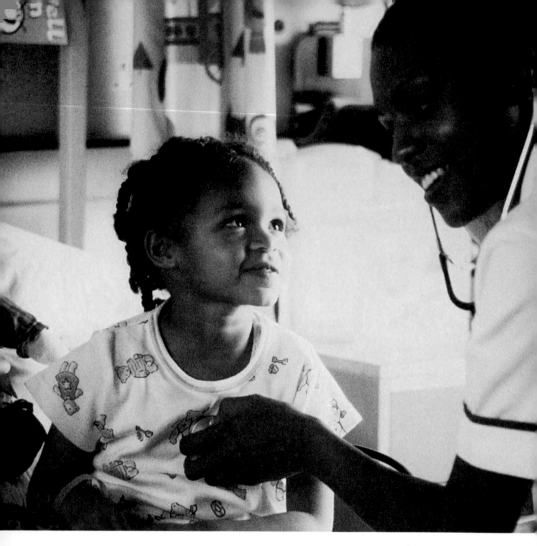

Your brain is so amazing that it can make your body do some things without you needing to think about them. You breathe without thinking. Your heart beats without thinking. Your body temperature stays just right. These are just some of the things your brain handles on its own.

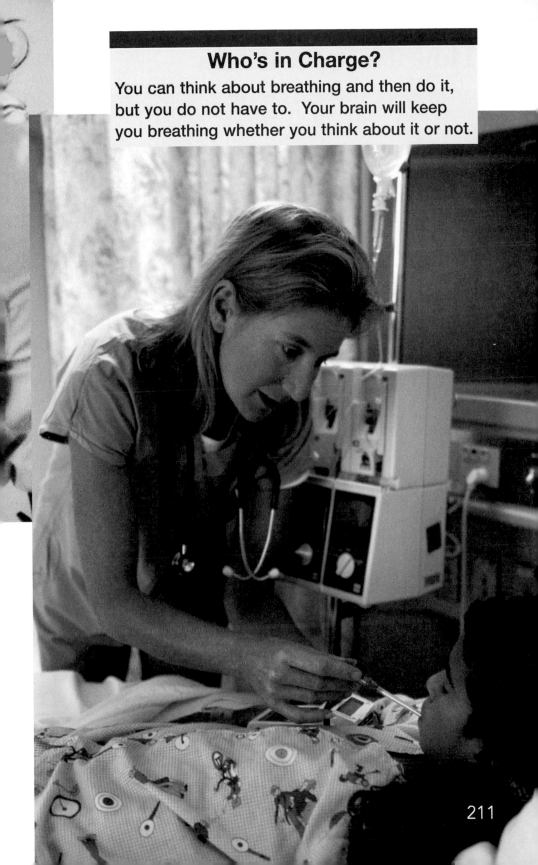

# Who's in Charge?

You can think about breathing and then do it, but you do not have to. Your brain will keep you breathing whether you think about it or not.

# How the Brain Works

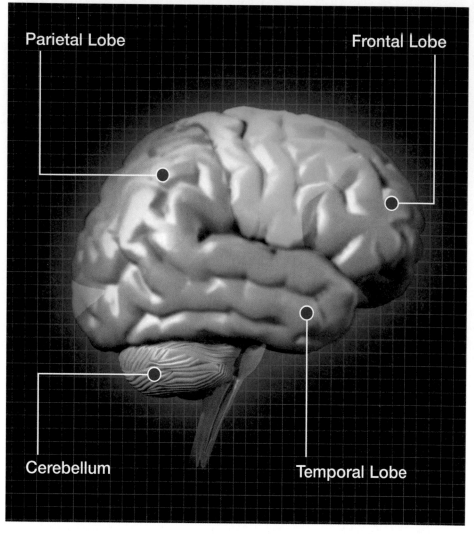

Parietal Lobe

Frontal Lobe

Cerebellum

Temporal Lobe

The brain is part of the nervous system. It works with the spinal cord and the nerves. They work together to control, balance, and keep the body, mind, and emotions in order.

212

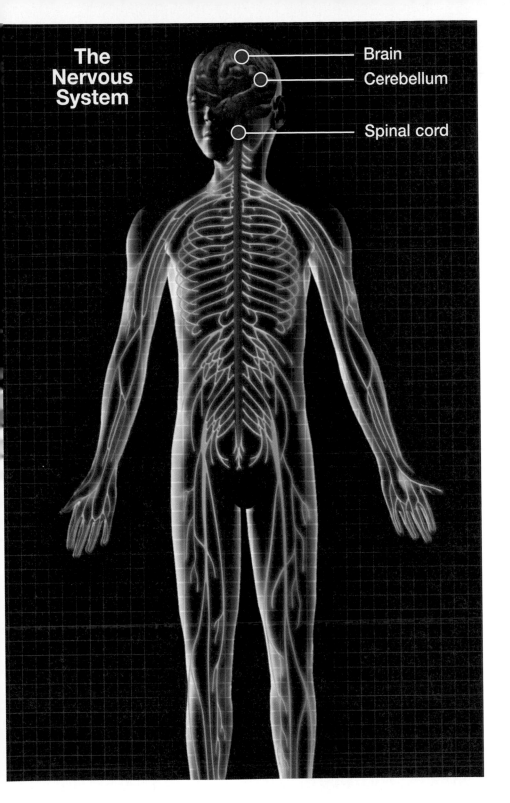

The
Nervous
System

Brain

Cerebellum

Spinal cord

The brain takes information from outside the body. Then it sends the information through the body, using the nervous system.

To get information, the brain uses the five **senses**: sight, hearing, touch, smell, and taste.

When you use your senses, you are using your brain.

To send information, the brain uses **neurons**. Neurons are nerve cells. They can be found throughout the body. They send messages to each other.

Each neuron is made of three main parts: **cell body**, **axon**, and **nerve ending**.

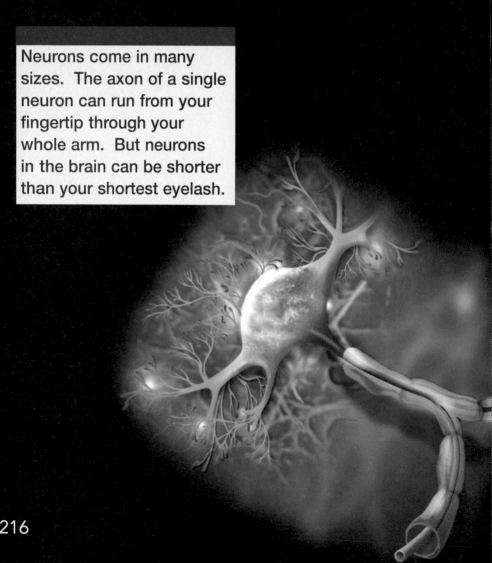

Neurons come in many sizes. The axon of a single neuron can run from your fingertip through your whole arm. But neurons in the brain can be shorter than your shortest eyelash.

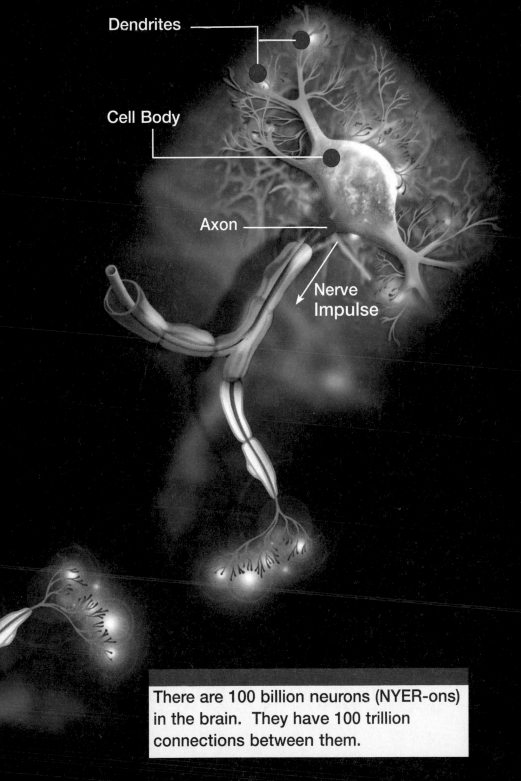

Dendrites

Cell Body

Axon

Nerve
Impulse

There are 100 billion neurons (NYER-ons)
in the brain. They have 100 trillion
connections between them.

# Parts of the Brain

The brain is made of the **brainstem**, the **cerebellum** (ser-e-Bel-em), and the **forebrain**.

The brainstem is in charge of the things we do without thinking, like breathing. It is also in charge of moving our arms and legs, digesting food, and getting rid of waste.

The cerebellum makes the parts of our body work together so that we stay balanced.

The forebrain controls our body temperature and our emotions. It puts together the information it gets from the senses. It holds our memories for us, and it lets us think.

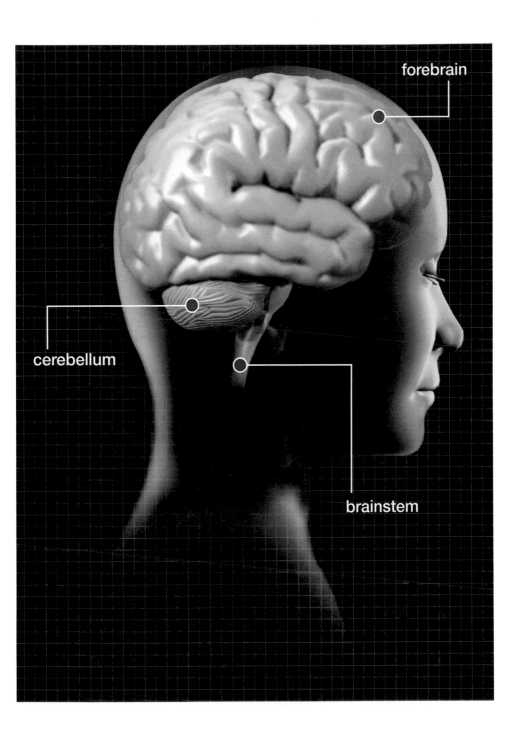

forebrain

cerebellum

brainstem

# Use Your Noodle

Has anyone ever told you to use your noodle? Have they said, "Put on your thinking cap"? These are just two of the funny names people use for the brain. They tell us to keep thinking.

It is important to use our brains when we want to do something. The

brain will tell us how to do it. It will tell us if it is right or wrong, and it will tell us if it is safe.

If you are not sure about something, just use your noodle! It will help you figure it out.

# A Healthy Brain

How can you keep your brain healthy? Everything in the body works best with good food and lots of water. Exercise is important, too.

How can you exercise your brain? Use it! Use it at school and at play. Think some new thoughts and try some new games.

Your brain likes to be used. So, use your brain and keep it strong!

# Glossary

**brain**   the body organ inside the skull that works with the spinal cord and nerves to control, balance, and keep the body, mind, and emotions in order

**brainstem**   the part of the brain that is in charge of automatic things, movement, digestion, and getting rid of waste

**cerebellum**   the part of the brain that makes all the body parts work together to keep the body balanced

**exercise**   body activity

**forebrain**   the part of the brain that controls body temperature, emotions, information from the senses, memories, and thoughts

**nervous system**   the system in the body made of the brain, spinal cord, and nerves that allows the body to think, remember, feel, and do things

**skull**   bones inside the head that form together and protect the brain

**spinal cord**   a column inside the back that connects the brain with the rest of the body

**nerves**   little sensors throughout the body that send and receive messages

# Travel in the U.S.A.
# THEN & NOW

## Maya Franklin

# Table of Contents

# On the Go

Where would you like to go? How will you get there?

You have many choices. You can hop on a train, drive along a highway, fly in an airplane, or sail across the seas. You can even go by foot. There are so many ways to travel!

But did people always have so many choices?

Long ago, when the United States was a new country, travel was very different from what it is today. There were no trains, no planes, and no highways connecting each city to the next.

So, how did people get where they wanted to go?

# By Land
## *Then*

The truth is that long ago people did not travel much. It was difficult and expensive to travel. People stayed near their homes.

Most people lived in small towns or cities. If they wanted to go somewhere, they would walk, ride a horse, or drive wagons or carriages pulled by horses.

People made or grew most of what they needed, so they did not have much reason to leave home. If their families lived far away, they would not see them often.

### Whoa!

Horses weren't the only animals people used for travel. Donkeys, mules, and oxen were ridden or used to pull wagons and carriages.

Most roads long ago were made of dirt. They were rocky, bumpy, and hard to travel. During wet weather, they became muddy and slippery.

In the winter, when snow and ice covered the roads, people sometimes rode in sleighs pulled by horses. Their sleighs did not have heaters like we have in cars today, so the travellers wrapped themselves in blankets.

### Hot Potato!

You probably like to eat baked potatoes, but long ago, people sometimes used them to keep warm. While traveling in cold weather, they sometimes put hot potatoes in their coat pockets to warm their hands.

# By Land
## *Now*

Today, many people drive cars and trucks. They ride on paved roads that cross the country and are easy to use in rain or shine. Automobiles today have heaters and air conditioners. People travel miles and miles in just a short amount of time.

**What Is an Automobile?**

An **automobile** (ah-to-mo-BEEL) is a type of transportation for people. Automobiles have engines and can be driven on streets and highways.

People can also buy tickets to travel
near and far.  Many cities have buses
and subways, and people can take trains

almost anywhere in the country. They just buy a ticket and get on board!

Not many people keep horses today for travel. Years ago, horses were the power behind land travel. Now, horses are mainly kept for sport and fun. Gas and electricity are used for power when traveling.

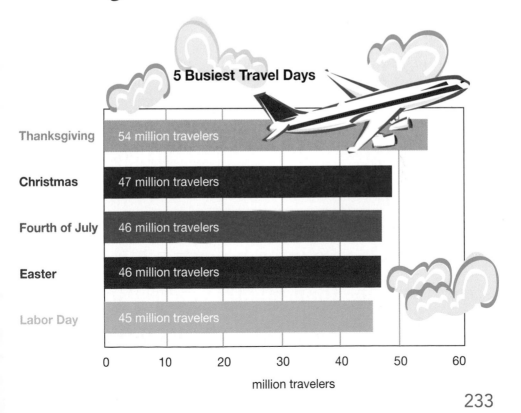

**5 Busiest Travel Days**

| | |
|---|---|
| Thanksgiving | 54 million travelers |
| Christmas | 47 million travelers |
| Fourth of July | 46 million travelers |
| Easter | 46 million travelers |
| Labor Day | 45 million travelers |

0    10    20    30    40    50    60

million travelers

A Colonial Frigate

Mast

Sails

Bow

# By Sea
## *Then*

People have been traveling by boat for more than 60,000 years. But the types of boats have changed over time.

**Stern**

**Rudder**

**Keel**

**Boats and Ships**

Did you know that boats and ships are not the same things? A boat is usually small with no roof. It is used to travel on rivers and lakes or near ocean shores. Ships are large and are made to travel across oceans. They usually have roofs and may have many different floors inside.

**Rudders** are used to turn a boat.

In the early United States, boats had sails, oars, and **rudders** for steering and movement. There were no engines. Only wind and muscle power made boats go.

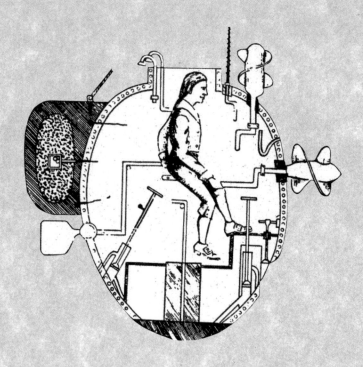

Lots of muscle power was needed for the first **submarine**! It was invented in 1776 and called the **American Turtle**. One person could fit inside. The person turned a crank to spin a propeller outside the submarine.

# By Sea
## *Now*

Boats and ships have many uses today. Some large ships carry supplies. Some carry people, and some boats are just for fun. People like to sail, fish, and race with their boats.

Boats today can go very fast because now we have engines. But some people still use sails and oars.

Ships today are usually much bigger than ships long ago. Cruise ships can take hundreds of people across the oceans. Navies have large ships to bring soldiers all around the world.

It is also easier for ships to find their way today. Now we have equipment so that sailors know exactly where they are and how to get where they are going. Long ago, the sun and the stars were all sailors had for directions.

# By Sky
## *Then*

Back when the United States was
a young country, you might see birds
flying in the sky but nothing else.  Hot-air
balloons and gliders would come soon,
but airplanes were still many years away.

The Wright Brothers manned the first successful powered flight in 1903 at Kitty Hawk. The plane flew for 12 seconds.

# By Sky
## *Now*

Now the sky is full of flying things. Airplanes fly from country to country. Helicopters whirl their propellers in the air. People fly in gliders and balloons just for fun. Spaceships soar to the moon and beyond.

# What's Next?

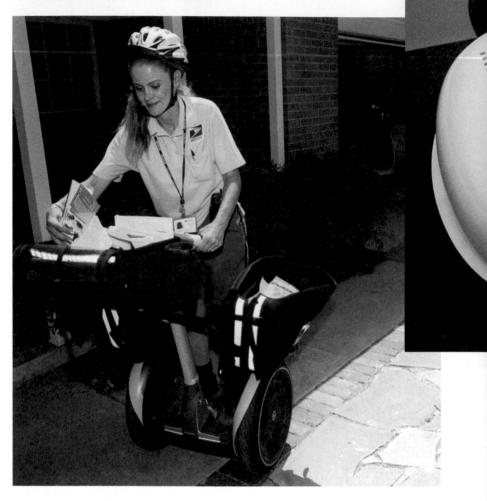

Travel has changed a lot over time, and there will be more changes in the future. It seems that if people can dream it, in time they can build it, too. By land, sea, or sky, anything is possible!

244

# Travel Inventions Time Line

Would you like to know how
travel has changed from the early

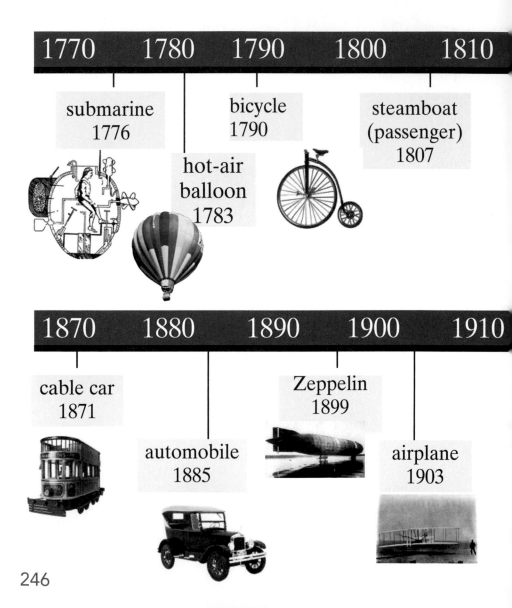

| 1770 | 1780 | 1790 | 1800 | 1810 |
|------|------|------|------|------|

submarine
1776

hot-air
balloon
1783

bicycle
1790

steamboat
(passenger)
1807

| 1870 | 1880 | 1890 | 1900 | 1910 |
|------|------|------|------|------|

cable car
1871

automobile
1885

Zeppelin
1899

airplane
1903

United States to now? Take a look at this time line. It will show you.

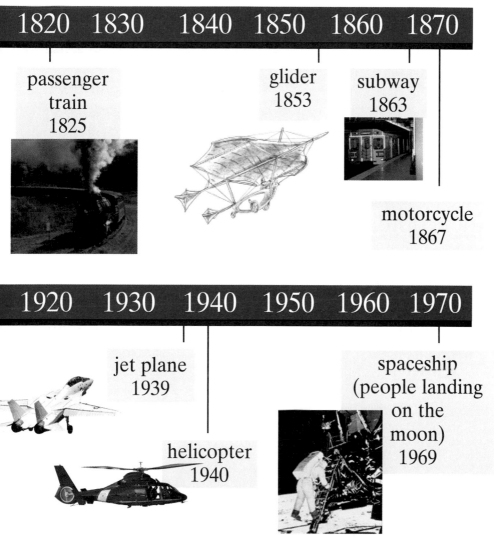

1820   1830   1840   1850   1860   1870

passenger
train
1825

glider
1853

subway
1863

motorcycle
1867

1920   1930   1940   1950   1960   1970

jet plane
1939

helicopter
1940

spaceship
(people landing
on the
moon)
1969

# Glossary

airplane

automobile

boat

bus

carriage

glider

helicopter

hot-air balloon

ship

sleigh

spaceship

submarine

subway

train

wagon